prayers for peace

robyn short

GoodMedia Press
An imprint of GoodMedia Communications, LLC
www.GoodMediaPress.com

Library of Congress Control Number: 2013934931
ISBN: 978-0-9883237-8-0

For the Peacemakers

Internal peace is an essential first step to achieving peace in the world. How do you cultivate it? It's very simple. In the first place by realizing clearly that all mankind is one, that human beings in every country are members of one and the same family.

— The Dalai Lama

contents

introduction

Peace is possible. In fact, if we are to survive as a human species on this planet, peace is inevitable. A friend once said, "It always gets complicated before it gets simple." The state of our human existence confirms this truth. We have complicated this human experience, and yet, it really is quite simple: the Bible calls for us to "Do unto others as you would have them do unto you;" Gandhi instructed us to "be the change you wish to see in the world;" Jesus taught us to "love God with all of our hearts, souls, minds and strength; and to love our neighbors as ourselves;" and the Buddha so wisely taught that "The mind is everything. What you think you become."

What we think, we become. What we sow, we reap. The neuroscience behind this spiritual teaching is that neurons that fire together wire together. In other words, as we think new thoughts we literally change our brains as new neural networks are created. As we change our brain through intentional thought, we change our actions. And as we change our actions, we change the world around us. The converse is also true: as we cease having certain thoughts, those neural networks disconnect and cease to exist; when those thoughts cease, the actions associated with them also cease. When we focus and meditate on peace, we rewire our brains for peace. So we think, so shall we be. As we turn our focus to a certain experience, we create that existence through our focused intentions. It is often said that "practice makes perfect," but when it comes to the brain, those in the neuroscience community know that practice makes permanent. And so it is that daily prayers for peace will bring about permanent peace in this world.

Every thought we have is prayer. The Universe is designed to set in motion that which we create, and our thoughts are the instructions for those creations. As we change our thoughts, the Universe will follow suit and change in response. We are indeed created in the image of God in that we are all creators. We are all endowed with the powerful gift of creation. God granted us free will, which means we have the ability to choose *what* we create, and we are *always* creating. We can choose to create peace, or we can choose to create separation from peace. We are granted the power to choose, which is the power to create the reality of our existence. As we choose peace, we transform. And as we transform as individuals, the world around us transforms in response. Peace is possible. It always has been, and it always will be. The choice is ours.

The prayers in this book will help you to be a vehicle for creating permanent peace in your own life and on this planet. As you focus your prayers, your thoughts, and your intentions on peace, your brain will rewire itself for peace. Your thoughts, and therefore your actions, will become peace. Commit yourself to a daily practice of meditating on peace, and experience the miracle of God's creative power as it unfolds in the world around you.

The prayers in this book are intended to be a framework to help you develop your own prayers that resonate uniquely with your own spiritual journey. Use the space provided in each section to personalize and recreate each prayer in whatever way you feel guided to do so.

Ask God—the Universe, the Holy Spirit or whatever name you choose to refer to our Creator as—to guide your thoughts and bless your mind as you spend time in prayer, creating a new and peaceful world. You are powerful beyond measure. Thank you for your contribution in making this world everything God intended it to be.

part one
peace of mind

mindfulness

. . .

Calm my mind and quiet my thoughts,
So I may listen and hear Truth.

Allow me to experience comfort
As I sit in silence, knowing the Divine is near.

Guide my thoughts and strengthen my faith,
So I may hear with clarity.

I surrender my fears and my worries,
Releasing all fear into the light.

As I go forth into the world each day,
May I carry peace and light into this world.

Today and every day.

release

. . .

In my moments of fear and separation,
May I remember the Divine's love.

As I breathe in slowly and consciously,
I invite the Divine peace to cleanse my mind.

I breathe in love,
Releasing all fear.

I breathe in grace,
Releasing all worries and misperceptions.

I breathe in forgiveness,
Embracing the peace of mind that is my natural
*   state of being.*

I accept what is,
Knowing that my life is unfolding according to a
*   Divine plan.*

comfort

. . .

Quiet my mind and restore peace to my spirit.
Dissolve all thoughts of fear and anger.

Allow me to experience the wholeness and peace
That is my birthright.

Restore my divine knowledge of Truth and
*   Goodness.*
Lead me to the path of Love and guide me on my
*   journey.*

May my peace of mind spread like the wind
And bring calm and comfort to all the world.

choice

. . .

I am grateful for the gift of free will.

From this day forth, I choose ...

Love
Forgiveness
Grace
Mercy
Integrity
Peace

For myself and for all those who are affected by my
   choices.

I choose to be the way of Truth and Light in this
   world.

growth

. . .

*As I experience the ups and downs of the cycles of
  life,*
I seek the lessons to deepen my learning.

*My intention is to bring my soul ever closer to the
  Divine.*

*May all my perceived failures and perceived
  successes be opportunities for growth.*

May all my losses be experienced as gains.

*May I always be grateful for the lessons my soul
  seeks,*
*And may I find comfort in knowing that my
  suffering is fleeting and my Joy eternal.*

*May my contributions here on Earth be a gift to all
  the world.*

transform

. . .

*I know the external world is a reflection of the
  internal.*

Transform *in me all that which is not peace.*

Transform *my thoughts so that they become ener-
  getic rays of love shining forth into the world.*

Transform *my words so that they are expressions of
  love for all who hear them.*

Transform *my actions so that they elevate kindness
  and eliminate suffering.*

Transform *my mind so that it is a mirror of the
  Divine reflecting peace on this planet.*

divine

. . .

May I boldly, audaciously, powerfully and coura-
geously proclaim my divine power as an expres-
sion of the Divine.

As an expression of the Divine, I am created
To be unconditional love.
Help me to extend love to all people.

As an expression of the Divine, I am created
To be a channel of healing power.
Help me to heal myself and all of humanity.

As an expression of the Divine, I am created
To be the manifestation of glory on Earth.
Help me to be an expression of creativity and
joy so that I may share glory with all of
humanity.

Robyn Short

As an expression of the Divine, I am created
To be peace on Earth.
Help me be the change that brings peace to our
planet.

i am

. . .

I have the power to proclaim that which I Am.

I Am Calm.
I Am Wise.
I Am Perfect.
I Am Complete.
I Am Ever-Changing.
I Am Love.
I Am Giving.
I Am Receiving.
I Am Forgiving.
I Am Merciful.
I Am Peace.

I bring peace, love and goodness to all living crea-
tures, and as such I am joyfully fulfilling this
mission each and every day.

part two
peace at home

temple

. . .

May this home be a temple of peace,
Where kind words are exchanged with ease.

May this home be a temple of grace,
Where loving actions continuously take place.

May this home be a temple of forgiveness,
Where all lessons are learned with tenderness.

May this home be a temple of patience,
Where we honor our similarities as well as our
    differences.

May this home be a temple of love,
And may all who enter feel the Divine presence
    from above.

home

. . .

*Bless our home and all who enter. May this home be
a beacon of light in the neighborhood, and may
love emanate as far as the eye can see and
beyond.*

*May our home be a safe haven for all who enter.
May our family, friends, passersby, animals,
and all living beings know that this is a house of
love.*

*May the peace that passes all understanding be ever
present in this home, guiding our thoughts, our
actions and our lives.*

*May all who enter this home know love, experience
grace, and share peace throughout the world.*

gratitude

. . .

I am grateful for the love that exists in this home.
It is an extension of Your unconditional love.

I am grateful for the laughter that erupts so joyously.
It is a reminder of all that is good in this world.

I am grateful for the quiet that settles over us each night.
It calls us to return our thoughts to the Divine.

I am grateful for our challenges and hard times.
They remind us of our strength and our fortitude.

I am grateful for the dawn of each new day.
It is an opportunity to renew our commitment to peace.

reminder

· · ·

Remind all those who live in this home that only Love is real. Help us to remember that only Love exists, even when it may appear otherwise.

Remind all those who live in this home that we are all of the Divine, and as such, we are all endowed with powerfully creative gifts. Help us to look past all illusions that may indicate otherwise.

Remind all those who live in this home to elicit loving behavior, even when we are most challenged to do so. Help us to forgive ourselves when we are unkind and to correct the errors of our thinking that caused us to be so.

*Remind us each and every day to carry Love in our
hearts, our minds, our thoughts and our actions
as we live together in our home and individually
in the world.*

part three
peace in relationships

beginnings

. . .

Peace begins with me. *Help me to always have
the courage to stand up for the Truth and to do
so with kindness, integrity, and acceptance of
others.*

Peace begins with me. *Help me to always be a ray
of light, bringing calm to the chaos that is so
prevalent in the world.*

Peace begins with me. *Help me to always take
responsibility for alleviating the suffering of
others; show me when and how to help.*

Peace begins with me. *Help me to be an example
of love in all my relationships, so that we may
all experience the Divine in one another.*

interactions

. . .

*I pray blessing on myself and all those whose lives I
touch today. May every encounter be a holy
encounter filled with opportunities for giving
and receiving. May I give with a pure heart and
receive with gratitude. May I recognize the
Divine in each person I encounter, and may
each person in turn recognize the Divine in me.*

*I choose to recognize that every interaction I have
today with another individual is an opportunity
for practicing peace. May my heart become so
skilled at peace that practice quickly becomes
permanent and that I may become a constant
embodiment of love in this world.*

mediator

. . .

*May I be a mediator for peace. May I bridge
conflicts with heartfelt communication,
allowing the hearts of all those involved to open
to divine healing.*

*Allow me to usher peace into every situation I
encounter today. May I facilitate open conversa-
tions with ease. And may all those involved in
conflict with one another grow to see and appre-
ciate the lessons the situation has to offer.*

*Help me to see that all conflict in relationships has
love at its core, even when it appears otherwise.
I trust that I am growing as a result of the
conflict I experience, and I am grateful for the
lessons.*

surrender

. . .

I surrender all negative thoughts and judgments of others. All thoughts are energy, and I choose the life-affirming energy of love and peace.

I surrender my expectations of myself and others, and dedicate myself to being in service to all people. I choose to seek opportunities of service in every relationship I experience.

I focus on the love and light that emanates from each person, for we are all expressions of the Divine. I hold compassion in my heart and in my mind. I recognize that every relationship is an opportunity for furthering peace on this planet.

part four
peace in intimate partnerships

love

. . .

*Please protect and uplift my Partner, surround this
person with glory and grace. May our commitment to one another grow stronger as we focus
our attention on love.*

*May our love bring us joy and uplift the lives of all
those who interact with us throughout our days.
Together, may we grow stronger in our commitment of service to one another and humankind
through our shared desire for peace.*

*May our love for one another be a catalyst of
healing for all those whose hearts have been
wounded. May the hearts of all people know
peace.*

union

. . .

When my Love looks into my eyes,
May they see unconditional grace.

When I look lovingly upon their face,
May I see a reflection of the Divine in their gaze.

When our hands are joined in casual touch,
May we never lose sight of the bond we love so
  much.

Guide and protect our love, so that we never become
  cavalier to this union we both hold so dear.

support

. . .

Each and every day support my Love and I as we encourage one another's compassion. Help us in our endeavors to always seek opportunities to nurture the good in one another.

Give us patience with one another so that we may develop and mature in our love. May we experience all the best of ourselves together.

Support us as we seek peace-building opportunities with one another and with all people whose lives we touch.

Remind us that ours is a holy union, and that the Divine is ever present.

protect

. . .

As my Love and I grow in our bond together, please
heal the wounded parts of our selves. Remind us
that our pasts created the present, and the
present is a precious gift.

May we cherish our journey in love together, and
remain focused on the present as we prepare for
our future.

May we grow as a couple, allowing the unity of our
love to blossom while holding true to the unique
individuals that we are.

May I bring out the best in my Beloved, and may
they bring out the best in me. And may we
support one another as we each experience the
complicated lessons on Earth that are designed
to help us grow.

Protect our love. Protect our union. And protect
    our individuality.

part five
peace in the workplace

flow

. . .

In all I do throughout the day, may my actions
create a ripple effect of peace. May my workplace
be a place of creativity and joy where peace is
experienced by all.

May the work I contribute always be of service to
the greatest good for all, and may my talents
and efforts always be given from my heart.

My work is my passion, and therefore I know it is of
the Divine. Guide me so that all my contribu-
tions are of service to others.

May I experience the reciprocal flow of abundance
that always occurs when our actions are in
alignment with our soul's purpose on this
Earth.

*Guide my actions so that I may contribute at my
highest level as I seek every opportunity for
creating peace in my workplace.*

oneness

. . .

*As a spiritual being having a human experience, I
know that all my actions and efforts are spiritu-
ally relevant. My home life, work life, personal
life, and spiritual life are aspects of one whole.*

*Guide me each day as I bring love into every aspect
of my life.*

May I always ...

*Do unto others as I would have them do unto me.
Love unconditionally under every situation.
Forgive unconditionally under every situation.*

gifts

· · ·

*My talents, time, efforts, and energy are all gifts
that I gladly give in service to the greater good. I
know that when I give, the law of reciprocity is
activated and the Universe supports me in
return.*

*I surrender my material desires, and dedicate my
work to the service of others. May I experience
the reward of seeing my contributions positively
creating shifts for peace in the lives of all people
and in my own life.*

*I am grateful for the talents and gifts bestowed upon
me. Help me to use these talents to create an
ever more peaceful world where we may all live
harmoniously.*

opportunities

. . .

*Each morning I awake to a new day filled with
many new opportunities for practicing peace.
May all my efforts and all my interactions
glorify You and deepen the experience of Your
love here on Earth.*

*May the work I contribute have a positive and
lasting impression on all those who experience
my efforts and contributions, and may the world
be better as a result.*

*May my heart, mind, and soul be nourished as I
consciously give of my talents. May love be at
the very center of all my actions, and may peace
ripple out from me into all the world.*

I acknowledge the blessing that each and every day I am able awake to a new day filled with opportunities for me to contribute passionately and purposefully to this world.

part six
peace in politics

leadership

· · ·

*Thank you for all the people who have selflessly
    risen up to serve and lead our states, nation,
    and world. May all those who do not hold the
    highest good leave their leadership positions so
    that another person may fill that space who has
    the desire to create meaningful, significant, and
    positive change.*

*May all our political leaders know that peace is
    possible and legislate from that knowledge,
    seeking to create a fair, equitable, and society in
    which all people may live in peace.*

*May the focus of our political leaders shift from
    power-centric to love-centric, from corporate-
    centric to people-centric, and from exclusive to
    inclusive.*

> *May peace fill our states' capitols and our nation's capitol so that the United States may rise to be a peace-filled nation.*

greatness

. . .

Bless our nation and help us to become a more compassionate country that seeks to heal the wounded and uplift the weak.

Bless our political leaders and help them to lead the United States with love in their hearts and the absolute good for all *people as the constant goal.*

Bless our congress and guide the congressional representatives to legislate with peace in their hearts. Guide our congressional leaders so that they create laws that lift all people from poverty, oppression, inequality, and injustice. May this country truly represent equality and freedom for all *people.*

Lead us toward compassion and heartfelt healing and away from punitive, power-driven political and judicial initiatives. May this country come to know greatness through peace and compassion.

healing

. . .

Heal the heart and soul of America. Guide our
country's leaders and citizens so that we may
become the embodiment of compassion and kind-
ness that is the cornerstone of true freedom.

Heal the hearts of all Americans, so that we may
truly see our Divine likeness in one another and
take action to lift one another from all forms of
oppression. Give each of us the wisdom to advo-
cate for and take action for initiatives that afford
all people equal opportunities as well as equal
rights.

Guide our thoughts, our hearts, and our minds so
that we choose to be of service to one another
and recognize that we are all *expressions of the*
Divine.

Robyn Short

> *May I be a light in this country and do my part in leading the United States out of the shadows of oppression and injustice and into the light of liberty and justice for all.*

power

. . .

I am powerful beyond measure, and I choose to use
my power to bring light into the darkness.

Through the Divine power that is invested in me, I
choose to be ...

A voice for those who are oppressed.
A voice for those who are wounded.
A voice for those who are weak.
A voice for those who have been forgotten.
A voice for those who are alone.

I choose to be ...

A voice for those who have lived in the darkness so
long that they have forgotten that they are *the*
Light.

Remind us all that we are extensions of Your Divine love and power on Earth.

part seven
peace in schools

safety

. . .

May all our teachers, administrators, and legislators come to know that every child is as unique as his or her individual fingerprints. May teachers, administrators, and legislators come to know that all children are endowed with their own special gifts. May the school environment foster individual growth, individual learning, and appreciation for the contribution of every student.

Surround our schools with love and grace, so that all children are safe and loved within the school environment. Bless our children with the freedom to learn without fear of violence.

Protect our children from those who have lost their way, and bring peace to our schools.

hope
. . .

Instill in our political leaders a commitment to creating policies that promote child-centered education for all children and learning styles.

May our political leaders be peace-promoting advocates of our public education.

Instill in our schools peace-building education.

May our schools be Lighthouses for peace and nonviolence.

Instill in all children a passion for peace.

May the children of today be the embodiment of peace and the peace-building leaders for a better tomorrow.

blessings

. . .

*Bless all the children of the world. Surround them
with power and grace. Guide their hearts,
protect their minds, and keep them safe from
harm.*

*Bless all the children in this nation. Surround them
with unconditional love. Return them to an
awareness of their innocence.*

*Bless all the children in this state. Surround them
with light. Remove the shadow sides of our
society from their minds, so that they may grow
and develop in the consciousness of peace.*

*Bless all the children in this city. Surround them
with joy. Lead them on the path of right-
eousness, so they may develop a love of service
and be of goodwill to one another and all of
humanity.*

> *Bless all the children in this home. Infuse in them*
> *the knowledge of love. May they be peace-*
> *builders in their schools and in the world.*

part eight
peace and the planet

restoration

. . .

*On behalf of myself and all of humanity, I seek
forgiveness for the violence that has been perpe-
trated on our planet.*

Forgive us for our waste.
Forgive us for our over consumption.
Forgive us for taking more than our share.
*Forgive us for our cruel treatment of the envi-
ronment.*

*Heal our hearts and minds in relation to the Earth,
so that we may consciously heal the wounds
that have been inflicted upon this planet.*

*Bring healing and wholeness to our earthly home,
and restore this planet to its majestic wholeness.*

> *I ask that today and every day, I see the way to creating peace with this planet. I seek how to live sustainably and peacefully. I seek a new way of being on Earth.*

cleanse

. . .

I am grateful for this beautiful, amazing, and self-organizing planet that is our home. May each and every person who calls this Earth home be faithful stewards of it.

Bless the air we breathe, and remove all toxins that pollute it. May each and every living being on this planet enjoy the pure, clean air essential for all living beings to thrive on this planet.

May we all do our part in returning this planet to its natural state of purity.

Bless all bodies of water — the rivers, lakes and oceans. May our water be pure and free from toxins, creating a healthy and fully functioning eco-system.

May we all do our part in returning this planet
to its natural state of perfection.

*Bless our land masses — the forests, mountains,
deserts, beaches and grassy terrains that make
up all continents.*

May we all do our part in returning this planet
to its natural state of peace.

sentient

. . .

On behalf of myself and all humanity, I seek forgive-
ness for the violence that has been inflicted on so
many animals living on this planet at the hands
of humanity.

Forgive us for cruelly holding animals in captivity.

Forgive us for cruelly testing and torturing animals
in the name of science.

Forgive us for disrespecting the animals' lives that
have been sacrificed for our nourishment.

Forgive us for the excessive and unnecessary
cruelty inflicted on so many farm-raised
animals.

Forgive us for violating the animals' lives that have
been taken for the sake of fashion.

*Forgive us for the violence inflicted on animals
living in the wild as a result of human greed.*

*Heal our hearts and minds in relation to the animal
kingdom, so that we may consciously heal the
wounds that have been inflicted on Your beautiful and awe-inspiring creations.*

*Bring healing and wholeness to the animal king-
dom, and restore all species and all animals on
this planet to wholeness. May we respect the
natural order of Nature.*

*Today and every day, I seek to create peace with the
animal kingdom. May the love I feel extend out,
creating a ripple effect across the planet. And
may my love be a part of alleviating the great
suffering to the animal kingdom that has been
caused by humanity.*

life

. . .

I am grateful for the beautiful, amazing, and self-governing animal kingdom that inhabits the land and sea. May each and every animal on this planet be restored with the dignity that is the birthright of all Your creations.

Bless the animals of the wild and of the sea.

May the divine order of Nature be restored through a deep and profound respect for all life on this planet by all people on this planet.

Bless the animals of the land and sea that provide nourishment to humanity.

May our natural symbiotic relationship with the animal kingdom be restored.

Robyn Short

Bless our pets.

May all domesticated animals be embraced
and loved by their human families.

*Guide all of humanity in restoring peace and
integrity to our relationships with all living
creatures on land and in the sea.*

part nine
world peace

interconnected

. . .

*As expressions of the Divine, peace is our natural
state of mind. Anything that is not of the Divine
is outside our nature. Peace is our natural state
of being.*

*Return us all to our collective Divine soul of uncon-
ditional Love, so that we may be born anew to
our peace-filled nature. Remind us all, each and
every day, we are all kinfolk. May we see our
similarities and cherish that which makes us all
individuals.*

*May all of humanity come to see that we are equally
responsible for one another, as we are all one.
May the peace that is in me extend out to all the
world, and may we all lift one another up with
the Divine knowledge of the God within us all.
The God in me, salutes the God in every person in
all the world.*

return

. . .

Lead us all ...

From illusions to Love.
From darkness to Light.
From separation to Unity.

May we all ...

Experience peace.
Awaken to unconditional love.
Be the source of all healing in the world.

Be with us as we all remain in service to humanity,
until we all choose to return to everlasting love.

Amen

co-creation

. . .

*I am grateful for the powerful gift of co-creation. We
all have the ability to perform miracles.*

I am grateful for ...

Peace of mind.
Peaceful homes
Peaceful relationships
Peaceful intimate partnerships
Peaceful workplaces
Peaceful politics
Peaceful schools
Peaceful planet

I am grateful for world peace.

about the author

Robyn Short

Dr. Robyn Short is the founder and CEO of Workplace Peace Institute, a consulting and research firm that brings peace and dignity to the workplace. She also works as a peacebuilding trainer, mediator, racial equity coach, and restorative justice facilitator. She is the founder and publisher of GoodMedia Press, an independent book publisher whose mission is to promote peace and social justice through books and other media.

Dr. Short is the founder and board chair of the Peace & Conciliation Project, a 501(c)(3) antiracism organization that brings communities together to address and repair the harm of racial injustice. Dr. Short has authored four books on peace building.

www.ingramcontent.com/pod-product-compliance
Lightning Source LLC
Chambersburg PA
CBHW030501100426
42813CB00002B/297